The Fire Cycle
Andrew Mossin

Spuyten Duyvil
New York City

© 2020 Andrew Mossin
ISBN 978-1-952419-23-2
cover: Michael Heizer's "Circular Surface, Planar Displacement Drawing," 1969, located at El Mirage Dry Lake Bed.

Library of Congress Cataloging-in-Publication Data

Names: Mossin, Andrew, author.
Title: The fire cycle / Andrew Mossin.
Description: New York City : Spuyten Duyvil, [2020] |
Identifiers: LCCN 2020024648 | ISBN 9781952419232 (paperback)
Subjects: LCGFT: Poetry.
Classification: LCC PS3563.O8858 F57 2020 | DDC 811/.54--dc23
LC record available at https://lccn.loc.gov/2020024648

For Monica

From a body's nature
From nature
Under whatever
Attribute
Follow
Infinite things
                        Louis Zukofsky, "[A-12]"

Contents

Moon Cycle   1

City Earth   55

The Fire Cycle   73

In Place of Conversation   81

Afterword   107

Acknowledgements & Notes   110

I

Moon Cycle

> Sing out the song; sing to the end, and sing
> The strange reward of all that discipline.
> W.B. Yeats, *A Vision*

I

The rain, orange in the sky
fades, down the side of a line

of orange, the sun
light when rain has

ended....This morning
re-creating that interchange

of language, apotheosis
of sound and color, light's movement

across sun cloud sky....

◆

Deepening
that could be like wind

run through the palms
of a stranger's hand.   Handsome

refractions, when the word spreads its
occasions southward....To venture

out late at night
passing under new moon

light   pale sheen of dew
across quadrants of lawn grass

passed through.

◆

Parenthetical…to say I
have come back   inside the drum

of language   a child
who learned place names

from a text of shadows.
Birth spacers   their residue of

color   'my own blood
a firefly among fireflies.'

◆

There is no distinction when
dreams come….direction the heart can

take…without deliverance
from its means. Wandering

away to return….
like glass placed between two forms

of light….Between
two phases of the moon to

enter the shadows lengthening.
across winter ground...

A theory of light
propositional   longitudinal

audible as fingers   tapping stone.

◆

To stay *here* though—
focus on *this* light

Who says we aren't?

◆

There had always been this position
of talking, then stopping, of failing

to listen, then listening, as if words
had become instruments of

obligation and denial.

◆

'We grow accustomed to the Dark—
When Light is put away—'

A trick in the voice—says its
name obliquely—obligingly—

written back for her—who
reads us as we read.

◆

My hands
brought to the surface of a lake

in mid-summer years ago—Geneva
from a distance—my mother's voice

moving inside itself, as if she
too were innocent of body

locational   episodic in water.

◆

Consciousness goes dark there.
Sentences left for another
                to complete.

Out of turn, she is turning
to hear us say   out of

turn   her face averted.

◆

Saying something to the mother
one had become—like laughter

through water—

        the routines

of one lifetime re-imagined
as prophecy.

And by nightfall

her voice fragmented
desolate   single in the night air.

◆

'Changes of light….in which we dwell'

Storm clouds across a lake
are storm clouds across a lake.

Another woman's voice historicizes
what's passed. One by one

the days relocate us. You and I
'are in the earth's turning'

Open to the changes that come.

Privileged   you say   to live
within these means.

◆

Shade where the ground
turned metallic

blue, a field of water lilies
propped up inside the folds

of light. Transfixed
like a figure outside himself, how

did he draw himself there, stretch
palms across the surface?

◆

That one becomes
two—at the end of something—

when we think back
blue peonies—to my eyes
  blue green colorblind—

 in a line from the
window & the empty white
  bulbs

  shiny in the cool June night.

◆

Forgetting who was there…

Bluing in memory. Daily goings
out. One hand follows

the other. Damp wind
when the day closes.

To see it pass…to engage
the porous clarities

of each day, part & parcel
we said, older

than we knew.

◆

Wind when the legs are tired.

Rain as the body awaits another day.

◆

A gift, then? A record of
reunion?   Simple

bird song that inhabits
a day without talk. Yellow

cast to the sky at sunset.
To recognize its form

all over again. Blue
black inside a network of

tree limbs.

◆

'As when the Neighbor holds the Lamp'

Windows she

said are made from
the inside out.

God lives there.

◆

Seeing the words come back   end of
day   there is the song coming into it

We are attendants
saying, 'like one wing

separated from another,' but
meaning   'inside one wing

separating another.'

◆

The way light passed

through my child's hand....

What shaded it, skin loosened—

separated from itself.

Ordinary light over ordinary skin....

◆

Nearer than I remember
Thoreau writing from winter of 1854—

'There is also some blueness
now in the snow—the heavens
being now (toward night—)
overcast—The blueness is more
distinct after sunset.'

as one reaches out
eternally to recover the
singular—

      public frame of light.

◆

What day is it? Same day
as each one before it   after.

A day at a time we say it's
daylight savings time.

What day is it? Same day…

◆

A line drawn from memory

as if one lifetime were product of
many. Gathering wood outside

in front of another's house
the color shifting orange to blue

along one side the bands
of sunlight moving us in their

direction   straight west.

◆

      A line drawn
on drafting paper—
      near the eastern path

leading back to carriage
      houses in winter…

There's little left of it
   West Virginia landscape

committed to memory   little
                       else.

◆

What is it about *this*
day—this
     hour I'm going *there* now?

Hearing it all pass thru again…Evening
sun across Martinsburg when we

drove back to the farm. Late summer
flowers passed on the highway. So

few birds I can recall though
one red hen came through the fence

at the property line & sat
not moving on the hot stones.

Someone along for the ride saying

         'We didn't see it'

◆

Wayward voice of a brother
I'd trusted to show me 'neither

sky nor earth'   cool underpass
where the weather came down hard

rain all afternoon long you could
lean into it taste its metal

'Can you find me here, can you
bring me my clothes?'

◆

At morning to go out among
the other kids….turning nine, turning—

Turning ten…
I was turning to remember how

I signed my name, wedged

my signature in the form of raised
lettering on paper. School sheaf.

Still seeing its blue line…red
down the margin. Writing in

line, left to right. Filling up
the pages.

◆

                        Earth's sun
light hidden by clouds.

Heavens sunk onto red canvas.

These regions where I lived…

Desolate   magical   where we
started from.

II

Earthly burden, burns
in the heart, mouth gone

tired, sleep takes the man's
mouth away. Lips, he says, are

gone, I have no mouth to
say or kiss with, come to this

place without touch, saying 'I
am without one or the other.'

At kindred's edge, placated by the
voices of Katyn and Anatolia, marking

time on my knees, the ease with which
days pass, grey folds, come back to

my heart.

◆

'Could I imply
what I could not name?'

Prayer as a channel of
light—passed through

palms—skin's shell.

◆

'I brought you back to re-
             store your sight'

Who was there….in the way of it.
I remember reading the story

of King Oedipus gone blind…What
he couldn't undo—

        a world   cut from sight.

◆

It is to repeat, sentence
after sentence, estranging the

body from what it knows. When
to go, where stain the ground

with red leaves, hear
tremors in a woman's lung.

◆

This lined piece of wood, breaks off, branch
by branch. Later to remember it as first.

 'I wait for the end of day, I wait
with my plants half-in half-out of their
pans, soil down my left hand, ridge
of skin that's caught, black loose
cut of square branch, held
                    out for viewing—'

Who was here?

Lay the book
aside, I said, where it goes on
is light.

◆

      Was it black
water in rain's cup, surety

of a vision left to
restore itself? I talked

myself out of where I'd
landed, walking in-

side a landscape less
real than imagined. And her

> voice said, 'this has shape and form, these
> are stones, let them sink into the waters
> with your body, let them form a shell
> of *tohu*'

◆

Light travels faster than

storm clouds
passing over us   I leaned into you

your voice bright
as a mourning dove's

late song   hovering inside the
frame of it   I was waiting for you to

unshed   unseal   blacken the ground
with shells of *tohu*   I was grieving

in the name of your return   that you
would come back this way

and seize the name I had
carried   so many days

before you.

III

Light when the body comes back
                                  to itself—

From above   saffron flakes falling

to the ground.

◆

More and more I hear the sound others made
when leaving….

in real time as the sun is real on the
window sill   & makes a crease

      on folded cloth
   laid across a chair
         half in half out of the light.

◆

I was not one but another   held in triadic
relation   as if hidden by parts of speech

kept from my boy self   the antithesis
of rain is light poured over slate

blue October, light….Hereafter
it is in this place no other—

crow cries   the emptying of their
vertical calls   moving out of our skin

into heavenly night.

◆

Reading Whitman against
winter light, lying down in bed

mornings to read all the way
through afternoon, as if position

were part of reception. 'The soil-
breaks apart in the hands—I will

remember its blackness forever'—
ground cover, the spring soil inside

a drum of flesh. And the slow leaking
light through the folds of skin.

How did we uncover what was lost
in flower, out of season, like an oar

drawn across the water, 'the flowers
turn toward the sea'   and accompany

us into darkness.

◆

The difference in what is
proposed   Light that is part of

a plan we can't see   Saying is
recognition and recognition....stands

apart from the boy   his arms
crossed over the shell of a

worn-out guitar case   left in a field
near Shepherdstown WV   the built-in

prospect of finding its music   against
all odds   fingers that can't play

back what the mind saw

◆

Here my father was going
back and I—his only son—
moving with him

on a street lined with chestnut.

◆

When the robin sings   I can say I have lived
here enough years to say the light is passing

through a winter stretch without color   the forms
of moonlight treebound   a line inside another line

until what my right eye sees crosses over
my left….

◆

To keep vigil here. Low tree
line of northwestern
            Pennsylvania

implicit in our thinking   as one value
                    of making   registered light of day.

◆

To house the spirit
world in this envelope of flesh   waking as we do

       inside folds of mercury light   embodied by its
       impermanence   outside
                          in

to travel back through   a scene caught
momentary   turning to light's
                      still object

◆

I can't remember   what restores sight
         clean lines of vision across

one field   another comes forward....

We are working out the design
across angular time   our dead layered within each
                       sedimentary layer....

◆

Shell of the green bird   cavern built of straw
light passed
      through wings of a hummingbird

from a rain squall   blackish at the root ends

shell and mantis
fern leaf and spider
      inhabit the lived world.

◆

Living earth time   where one goes
forward   it is enough light to see   day
                       by day to see

red ochre
        garlands of peony and thrush root

blended by the hands of a stranger

◆

When the waters go dark   hear the rasp
of bird song again,   shell by shell   in a concordance
        of river music   rising from the tree line.

◆

Red hen
by the post was
sitting by the

red post a
hen resting
near a post

moving into
the light
evening

light spun from
radiant splash
of blue

down the
hen's red
body.

IV

A bird, frightened, rests atop black
iron...like a shell poised to drop

into the sea. Tide falls, air
blackened by haze....fearless

sparrow sits, rescues its mate, secure
in where it will next go...The observed

world: irises in a row, canopy of shade
drawn across the rows of tomato and dill

One is less able to draw conclusions
from these acts of watching

as if ritual were its own end, its own
surface of recall....Paints a world

inside & out, bordering the recollected
in this time, now that.

◆

For Sobin poems
are prayers....the epigraph

like a stutter of smoke
moving into the light.

I rested there once
saw myself in his language

perhaps a child coming
back from school

weighted by blue
charcoal, the implicit

tag of daylight, left
in the open….

◆

        (1966 springtime)

To learn how it must have been, disclosed, not yet
understood, that the woman was sitting in plain
view, morning light that came into its own, a partition
between mother and son, her hair coppery tied
in a bun…near her left hand a small piece of paper
where in two columns she'd written the names of plants
flowers trees

    As daylight that broke across the fence

  white posts in damp spring clay

    dogwood & pussy willow

        each held in view.

◆

    Downstairs where the water was running
        in the dark with it she was hanging
    laundry, dropped to her knees

on the wet floor, a skinny piece of rope
        she said, 'loosen this for me,' so that I got
  hold, I

                wrapped it in my palms & gave it

                back to her

And the light was

        low to the ground   basement light

        impervious to its source   low level light

        with a hint of yellow   & behind it fenced in

        our garden of dill thyme mint & the first

        roses of the season.

V

*To dream of the eternal
waters, as rivers are
           flowing east to west—*

Had trees lived where the
days were left aside….

Reading back the days
when forces of another nation's

army were defeated, recorded
by Du Fu in the 3rd month of 759

> 'But house and village a wilderness now,
> near or far are all one to me.
> And always I fear for my mother, sick so long
> five years buried in a mere ditch of a grave.'

And stone was cut
at the quarry & earth

restored by
fresh-rushing river water….

◆

           Where the poet rested to write—

'Four directions, no peace, no safety'

           The long living
     passing our home by the
                ancient river—

tree limbs where the bodies
      recede to shore.

◆

I don't pray but
ask for forgiveness—
      Let my body

find safe passage

      through a mouth of water.

◆

The emptiness

of our hands at
Potomac's edge.

◆

      Silverweed along the edge
where water lies at a crossing
          sand inside wet fields

      of strawberry, hints of
mint, moved through our palms—

      This encyclic
of sense memory, word of
          mouth, strands of
      marsh cinquefoil

gathered up narrow by the water's edge.

◆

    And if Iris had picked
goldenrod in October
        where light was sharp

    Her eyes might have caught
asters standing amid blown
        tops of roofs

    drenched in seawater
from ancient aqueducts
        renewing their fill.

◆

    Working from the book
of wildflowers
        to read the world

    of dark 'basal and lower leaves'
'cordate and slender petioled'
        rising in a low wind

branching sweet heaven's gate
        row upon row.

◆

    And to see them
back in bloom—

    burning discs of tender
        Horseheal—

      heart-shaped   involucres

           plaited discs of yellow
                    St. John's Wort sloping

              across empty pavement.

  ◆

           'I cannot claim to
have wisdom from what I saw'

                    Indian cup   birth flower

       so many have seen them
                       rainless at sundown

                        raised in prairie light

       yellow ray flowers
              barricaded outer bracts
          of broadly ovate
                        involucres.

  ◆

          To keep our mind
                    clear—

       Falling into each crevasse

       Dear Heliopsis….

VI
for Ryszard Mossin 1910-2003

And if language stops?

Counting the days
when they are the same.

To return among these hours..

    Here? where there is no
  more liberty than what
this time provide?. Earth

    loose in the hands—
comes loose in
      the hands.

◆

Because it does end—one
way or the other, as you

said, 'you never know
what will happen.'

◆

Recurrence is possible
in the simplest form of its

understood public affect—

    the days go without
notice, the pile-up of
      sensations—

a border separating there from nowhere.

◆

   Above is as it was
understood—a metonym for
         being.

◆

'Śladami' which loosely translates

in the footsteps of

Following one man, my father.

There's no relation inside
        or out—

A gathering

where he's gone—separate
soul at rest—

   'the wet snow in our hands…'

◆

As if we traveled across
to render his body
visible again.

Target language of so much we say—
in translation coming & going
out of where we are.

'The dead, awaiting these visitors,
ready their workshop,
plane themselves down.'

◆

He kept
no journal, wrote sometimes

he couldn't sleep, the ice
between his hands, white writing

he called it, shadows of
thought—

   Russian winter he saw his first
eagle   cross into the wind

              & ice on his tongue.

◆

'If I'm tired I say
      sleep is what
   is coming—'

Dense night sky   Orion's belt

The ancient view...

◆

Śladami...

Carried him away from himself
as one man became two...he said he

was reading….in an unpeopled land
he said he was freed to return

without a brother….he saw nothing
of the landscape….Days & days

it was winter…

        'Here in the
garden, under a cherry tree or two

were crops' he remembered

'wheat, corn, beans, barley…
     even shrubs and flowers'

from *Pan Tadeusz*.

◆

And if—
not now—when?

    'At the foot of a chessboard of small fields
    ran a stream, with huge maize plants growing
    along it, occasional sunflowers, and green
    plots of thick grass or clover.'

◆

A road moving up through Bajgiran
blue clouds   on paper

my father's eyes
the singularity of his

face as it reappears to me
in the words of Czapski—

'Here by the winding
stream   August

after the burning summer
the green of the meadows

and the white-trunked poplars'

◆

       'The dead do read us'
    as one reads objects
            in a night storm—

moving across the sky—

    Memory of a lifetime
  built to last
        a few days at best.

◆

Back & forth—

we're here where he
isn't—or staying

back to hear his
voice   animated   severe

several.

◆

There is the actuality
of time—

      Bajgiran….rain

as it must have fallen…cool to his skin…

In this complexity of retrospect
what is it I am asking

      one father to complete?

    Our corner of southeastern Pennsylvania that tilts
        away from the living…

      Rocks in a garden bed…a cycle of lightning to the west….

◆

Paradise invades the senses….

Not death's certainty
but the position one takes

inside it….

◆

To say as Du Fu did   'fish and dragons
         were here at its first creation

        water-chestnuts and caltrops, same in present
        and past…'

Isolated in what was once here—

Let us 'built a thatched cottage
for this poor old body.'

◆

'I remain fixed
on myself. I magnify myself to what extent?'

The opportunity to sit without chairs
in the late light

       of this afternoon…books
       where a man's body was.

◆

As though through it all
we could say their names again   a little night

one by one   to say their names
'bedstraw' 'eyebright'

 inflame the eyes   as a woman
walks out of the garden

among the late blooms of zinnia & marigold
their folds of color….

'There is the universe and one is in it.'

VII

Storm channels
churning east by southeast
     out of the Lehigh Valley
    summer lightning
         splitting elm & oak

    hard rows of wood
    from the wind harvest.

◆

Hard to travel out
beyond where one is.

Habit's taskmaster. Scenes
that are localized—

    mound of earth from
  a tree stump, piled high below
       my window

This time tomorrow is
this time, tomorrow.

◆

The curiosity is unevenly
    spread, not events but their
  eradication, as if the spell
      were applied to bodies
    capable of little else, eased

  onto wet earth, mounds of pine
   cones, encircling their
       nude limbs….

◆

'Approaching death,' Williams writes, we are
        unable to distinguish ourselves from
     those we sought to love

the indeterminacy of location   that
        our geography root us in persons
     their irrecoverable addenda: clothing, books, objects
          gathered in a pile

returned to their owners.

◆

YET, WE ARE BROUGHT BACK…

     Letters from a woman I
never met— her vision less certain
        than my own—60 years later.

     A lifetime become tributary, broken
force, the rushing out of time, as if each
        abided the separation in isolation.

◆

A form of prayer, silent
   absolute, as if language
 had come from the gods
    weighted down by logos

   in this 'heaven of composites'
        we are so many who come after.

◆

      Angelic wing, tributary

    tide, the shortness of breath

        that comes from long days

     spent near water.

◆

Base nights or we are
  less cautious with time—

bordering the throw-away years
    a system of sight-reading
      to enter the music
  at a glance, see its notes rising
         in ritual mode of thought—

To come after is to raise
     one's eye, curious
   across our days.

◆

       Where we are
   in the whittled-down place
      in full sunlight of afternoon

   To reckon with one woman's dying
   absence for which there is
      no answer—

  'We missed
      even bread,' she wrote from Athens

28.11.95 'I go three times a year to
my village—I cannot visit more
because I must work.'

◆

The sea, I might have asked her, when
did you find the waters
near or far, when did you
reappear, small in the

local eye?

◆

To afford a life….seasonal
  efforts, to maintain
    what's there, what can be
    contained in one room…

Summertime she is sitting
  at the café, reading Cavafy
 poring over the pages, she
    is sitting alone, in the light, with

  her book open to such pages.

◆

As reunion rests, light
from the hills above Thessaloniki
she can't keep count of
our days away, months and years
out of count—

>   Venus, she says, your moon is rising
>   and the days we have
>   are uncountable.

◆

Cavafy, a century before
had written—

> Of voices, 'imagined voices, and beloved, too,
> of those who died, or of those who are
> lost unto us like the dead.'

In her dream of his arrival
       in Piraeus, 30 years later she
  would envision
             his name stenciled in water
       beneath her window.

◆

'Sometimes in our dreams they speak
      to us; sometimes in its thought
    the mind will hear them.'

As near the Delaware
   dreams of my first mother merged
 with the tide moving
           south to Atlantic.

◆

As I returned to read
from Whitman—

  'The beautiful spiritual insects! straw-color'd
  Psyches! Occasionally one of them leaves his
  mates, and mouths, perhaps in a straight
  line in the air, fluttering up, up, until literally
  out of sight.'

  In the water's nest
 a clear light, bracketed by
   sediment mudfall white ribbon

◆

Adrift or afar?

Rising early to read
what I'd written yesterday, how to say
   the necessary next thing?

Span of years, elongated, topped
branches of fallen trees
  legendary span of their
    ring cycle. Breath

is like skin: freshest
at birth….

◆

To locate oneself
here, among these partitions
   day brings new day
  light new light—

Orphan music is a form of
homage, lifted, idiomatic as
  color forms a ring inside one's
    hand, proffers

an emptiness without return.

◆

   'All appears
as if seen
     wavering through water.'

The lines augment what has already
happened, objects that became
   matronymic in my time

now shift, open up, lose their resonant
edges….

◆

   Water moves in a channel across
my line of vision, rainfall from the sudden
    August storms.

In another hour, the sunlight will
   crease the landscape, perforate
     its surface.

To know what we have to know
   about our own death
     is to be located here

in view of the sun, an arc of light
   orange then pale
     yellow, opening across

my field of vision.

◆

'Here is my hand,' the woman
             says from another world—

        'Take it so you
                    are ready.'

VIII

All this light
may remain, we say the
           starvation tune

     is apt, the red
skirt, bell of sound, low
           song of the mourning dove

     in evening…We
untravel this distance, this cross
           light, river

     where the hand goes
still, River Is that becomes Was—
           as we turn toward

     snow at the river's mouth
woods covered in jade frost
           our small boat floats away.

◆

The politics of light
    is the parallelism
  of experience—

To inhabit the same
    space, heartfelt
  spirit, build the

habitual record out
    of mental time
  scarcely visible

       to the naked eye, lived
            apart from sanction
        or recollect

this revenue of water & sky.

◆

        Not out but
toward—

Your decade weathered
        or overly read
    for what it couldn't

reveal: 'In the eyes dream'
        Rilke writes of his
    father as a young man

revealing the long space
        between yearning
    and fatalism—

inert as a wheel of red
        clay, the forehead
    tilted back, shaved

neck—cool
        to the palm.

◆

        We are waiting
        you said
            for disappearance.

◆

Earthly colors that fade
  where water is ageless
 our pathways through
    peaches and plums

recognizable calamus isle.

◆

   And light 'moves on the north
sky line' and 'across the full ornamental
    braids' of his uniform

   My father's hands, at ease, resting
level with his jacket's hem
    forest green on blue.

◆

And all of it
September or the earth
  is resting between

seasons, sumac & oak
inside a ring of light
  unimpeachable

from our window every
branch is resting between
  fronds of red

uneven color. The history
of this perception is
  radicalism's shadow—

cut from wind sheer, the rain
isn't yet a presence

◆

      In the *Pekaj*
we bend among its naming for days
              a flower wind shell

     inside circle, pin broken
from its cloth, loose on the ground
           red as amber shell

      scattered at the river's edge.

◆

'Mouth is a sign' we read
        for the first time our hands
    filled with flowers from the

          cracked river, come back to haunt…

◆

Skin is emplaced here as

    Water lily serpent wind quetzal serpent

are pillaged, in the turning mouth
      of river light, cloth through the
    hands, writing on the sides of

      our human body….2 days can bring 12…

Overcast, in the breaking dawn
        to reveal the power of hands

writing their way back to

        Deer   Pride   Artisan

◆

    What combines
    appetites—

        surrounding our

physical space   paratactic light

folds   writing on the flesh

of animal skin   our frightened

soul accompanied   by mouth

rasp sand wax   underneath a pillar

'the sound of the word'   inverted

4 more days bring 12

◆

    Grey scale of the wind
that rises behind us....

        Seventh morning song rising....

◆

>If this is
>rope, the river
>
>can't be
>far from
>
>here.

◆

We put our heads together.

We lay these things side
by side…in the magic waters

of Chesapeake & Delaware
we chart the way

'circling in the eddying air.'

◆

A black lake the seventh
to be seen, Saturn in the

red evening sky, tilts
our heads upward…

◆

>>We remember we are
>in company….the words are not
>>>our own…

A score of 6 days brings 8
         Writing on the walls
in this month of no destruction
             we are keeping summer

     with us, pale where the mouth
is discretionary, to reveal the white latex
         of its flower

     that gives off this scent, incarnadine
black in the red car with jewels
         this bright arc of
                winter light.

◆

     Scar wood, pale
soft fig, cool cypress
         under red moon

     A name threaded
from many—
         black lake

     Seventh moon.

◆

     And death and spirit

     are split down the middle....

As birds hover in the myrtle tree.

         Outside our window a doorway
     cut from fir needles

Give glory its due.

◆

Light at the river's edge.
Delivered to its basin
              a falcon's wing

broken from a column of reeds
                      enters heaven.

5 January to 28 September 2019 / Revised March 2020

II

City Earth

And then the earth arose because of them; it was simply their word that brought it forth. For the forming of the earth they said "Earth."
Popol Vuh (tr. Dennis Tedlock)

To arrive at this place of numbers without sun
rotating on a limb of catalpa

freighted wind from the south
opening oneself to what is to come.

Here is visualization on the red
map a rope passed among strangers

who read the calendar of days
for signs of return.

Here is relic sign imparted to the last
departed on the Street of Death

where their names are written in sand.

◆

The dead are waking beside us.

To be consumed by the rhythms of the desert is to be
uncovered on pallets of straw and magnesium

to be surrounded by hawk flares
in a sky constructed of magnesium.

Here in the beginning of a chapter titled 'new beginnings'
the arousal of shame as the human objects are set

into the ground….A depth of shadows mechanically drawn. Here is our signature

etched in larkspur and bone.

◆

The dead are waking inside a grid of poplar and granite.

Solitary practice inserts itself in this desert of larkspur.

One remembers solitude of rain's iridescence.

Red stone covered over in sand.

The murmur of skin underneath tented wind.

Animated by what is present / octagonal shape of star.

◆

We are celebrating the birth of moon on a slow falling lake.

Let the surrender come to you in calligraphic bursts and spiral

                      jets of granite dust on red clay.

◆

Anthracite flame from inside its canyon

Lizard & mule deer.

Cave city where no city is.

Dehiscence of land flow & flower beginning

on a surface of yellow flint.

  Blue phacella and desert willow....

◆

Coyote dawn.

  Puma light from the west.

Each Silver Slipper...

Black mesquite's copper scorpion.

Heading toward its line planted in desert grass.

Dark where coyote strayed....

Creosote on black lines that form a creosote circle

looped by wild honed toads

  a basin of red light...torn by floods

  from Pangaea's mouth.

◆

Herons & centipedes moving in unison

    across deposits of molybdenum.

◆

Noon's captive
toads flamingo vultures

huddled at an impasse
blind timber rattlers

Seven as a rite of passage

No locale
No closure

◆

Frontier's cinder ruins across U.S. 1
Smooth ellipsis of crow cry

Pine kill on petroglyph hill
Gnomic rasp of shifts

Draft shale mounds
of bleak iris

Heads of seagulls
atop basalt nuclear stockpile

Lifting a javelin's head from desert floor
built on a theorem of antelope.

◆

To drop down knee-level
on soft desert grass

A seeker built of skin & muscle…

◆

Nimbus of pine & mule deer

Tracking the self out of hiding

On desert grass jaguar's lair

Encamped on horizon's elbow

Sage brush where sea once was

Ornamental bromelias of forest

Anemone fires across blue cuts of sky.

◆

Hinged city horizon
that rests inside the bank of cactus light.

Wave cavern
Bridge where light escapes

A pattern of after lifted out
High inside heron's ridge

Locale's circular scale
Planted over ridge look-out

Indention's crow flight
looping over city dirt slide

lift of its granite Braille
hidden inside basalt's cut-through.

◆

Raven wing

Meteorite show high in the western night

Isolated cusp of desert canyon

Pools and spills down the hills

Human bank of rock

This nether space of signs

Mortality's episodic drift

'My leg became the tool'

Drawn line cut into new earth

Lined earth drawn over

Dissolves of Snake & Crab.

◆

In patterns form exists apart from the form

      Ossuary built city sky

Lock of grass

      Gnomic bone that has the meat inside

Lift of its bromeliad flowers

      Like skin dripped in fat

Ocean wood where it loses form

        Skin's alembic cull

Signs of sky's house

        Cut from skin's viscous meat.

◆

Sun bark

Earth's declivity   A bend inside its arms

Torso's somber decal

stripped of ground to give up ground
lake's traveler blind for evening

Javelin hunt
where skin is tight

held together by rope's coil

And the circle is a graft on earth's skin.

◆

Gave ground under the Seven Macaw

Drift's alembic core

Skull weather
writing itself out

snaking through wind's open harness

Blind peristalsis
Leg line on desert floor

Where yucca flower is part basin part
Orphic crown

Came under the spell of the Seven Macaw
Venus & Scorpius

rising in the east.

◆

Junajpu's blowgun

black tint of its spill
blown into nance tree's hideaway

sky ink drawn to their lair
nance tree's scorpion rising

from sky's water released
loose wind heading east

rising above sky water's shell.

◆

Foehn wind heading west
    arch of red desert dust   highway's barren
cellular mark   sundown's lure   caught
                          fish at the sky's edge

◆

Loft where loft isn't space anymore.
Position as one becomes it.

A form of writing across earth.
Cross where the lettering fell down.

'There is this route…this leg
that leads backward in possibility.'

White splinter of sand circle
over circle in this exercise

of repetition finding
the crow line back through

cactus veins.

◆

No utterance when
our dead rest apart from shelter.

Praying before dawn…

Drawn
backward into abyssal core

of red sun…Dart's morning shower
signaling blood

from the hyena's call
a ring of owl feathers

perishing beneath a ledge
of mountain ice.

◆

To imagine what wasn't here before…

Mill grass and sedge weed
lunar eclipse dense white sky's

carryover light deepening
noon's carrion caught in dense grass.

Moon rises where sun was
Small green space cut into cubits

Black dots on wet grass

Arriving before dawn without
tools arriving inside a drum

of color and light
without tools inside a drum

sealed from within…

◆

Cactus flower & peach blossom.

Remembering what afternoon was
when it broke under teal rain's

branch…Five storms in one
day…Fire from inside the canyon…

One was keeper of the White Road

One was protector of the Black Road

Saq B'e and *Q'eka B'e*

◆

Hearthstone's rising across horizons' edge...

Birthbone resting on desert floor

Ground cover where light is pleated
   Nude wing of falcon
Rising in the east
      Ground severed from its twin...

Falcon where the east is scorpion

         A tree sliced from a bed of coral
    Loose bed of gravel
         pouring down silt

      Riverbed's cracked jaw

◆

   Blown over
      Wind's high rise   Crossing a T
Earth pyre where star descent begins
       Loose nimbus of creation's bed

Black July when the heavens open

        Storm rock on cold
           ash urn.

◆

Frontier sky   crisscrossing September's arc
    Hill bank shell of seeds
   Limbic soul that meets its
       Black Road

◆

Under White Sky
limping migrations' trail

Long line of dirt
piled high 300 feet in diameter

◆

Gave tongue to unchanging definition—

    raised serpentine

    light from the desert floor

    raised silver scar

    in earth's canyon a passageway

    cut from rainfall at evening.

◆

Sky's mastaba form   Burial's slough site

Wall cut from wall   Urns poured square
90-degree walls

Earth sliced from earth
Piled arc

L winged
columns resting on earth.

◆

And he lived in a dream of
               Chicen Itza.

Serpent scale in one long arc.
         A trace of the real
    Suspended across upper columns.

Like a trance lifted from its sky port
took itself for a dream lived underneath

◆

Rock's shelter port's linear cut
          drawn from earth   sky   red serpent

         Head of the snake built from a drum of nails
Arc of the snake's mouth

Drawn in a line of earth   Snake like a line drawn across the wall

            Head & mouth   built on a mound of red.

◆

Earth extracted from earth
pool shine of mule deer   paper tracts

Loose limbed where 3,000 feet could be cut from earth

Masked a design by rock's ridge

◆

Rode it out to hear its ceremony
blacken on wide grass edge

Dusk where morning isn't
Serpent slipped across the hand of the owner

Like a dream of Alnitak
 cut from light Orion's belt   sky's seam dipped in
                                              antelope blood.

◆

Rocks have their spirit.

      Quint mule tracks blind yucca Borealis split.

        Took spirit for a name inside O.

Hurricane season when the rocks disappear.

      Desert rock flooded by Dipper light.

◆

Namesake's query where earth sends it back.
      House bright in sun. Columns weight.

Burial house of bright sun's arc.   Scorpion
rising in the east.
      Western sun descending over L.

    Sky's crevasse metal rain
      drum slickening earth's spine.

◆

'Earth earth soft earth'

Venus at rest
over dried crust of desert

Dark beams laid over clear pine rock
red sky built of white

pools and spills red in red light of sun
these depressions of hand and eye…

◆

The work gone within two weeks

lifted out of earth's cavity   rain makes a wash

      Teal down the hills' spine
red bands of light that lift   renewed volumetric

            scale by scale

                grooved by absence.

31 October 2016-2 January—22 May 2019

III

The Fire Cycle

> One morning I looked out in the garden, the boars were digging. They were wild. You can resettle people, but the elk and the boar, you can't. And water doesn't listen to borders, it goes along the earth, and under the earth.
> Svetlana Alexievich, *Voices from Chernobyl*

1

One day instead of a village you have
an empty field   the most basic features of

a field without color or contours   as if to
remember the sky when the fires

burned east to west   a rim of shadow
paralyzing sight   reflections of the sky

on wet panes   the nimbus of ash
forming along the red rectangle

square situated inside a tunnel   of white
ash separated from the sky   as if fire

had become the object of field   Field & fire
are objectives of understanding   as if to instrumentalize

vision the way a fire burns   a line of fire
burning at the periphery of sight   the hollow

limbs that are brought into view   radioactive
logs in a line   silver where the branches

point east to west   across the horizon the pointed
limbs in a field of grey metal   one line after

another lit from within   white scar of light
red on the mud opening out.

2

To recover the species   re-discover its position
in the landscape   enter the space where it transforms

its transition from one state to another   Bird that forms
an image in mind   *Hirundo rustica*   barn swallow that

establishes relation to a before   this balance
one achieves between before & after   the barn swallow

and its history in a before   native to the
region so that it embodies its history   seasonal bird

re-presented in a structure of change   One counts
mutations of the germline in percentages

2/10 to establish changes to the germline   a record that is at once
observation of change and a document of

transformation   Swallow that flies into the morning sky
albinistic feathers on its head   throat and beak

tail feathers that are asymmetrical   bent tail feathers
that become signs of its mutation   a site of transformation

the body of the swallow   transformed
in the span of a decade   quietly coming into view

a mutation of blue and brown feathers   albinistic
markings of head and throat   acts of change

marking the territory of swallow   a dimension
of aftermath   in the singular form

blue brown changes of color   scattered rain light
down the swallow's tail feathers.

3

Whatever comes in sleep enters   a slow trail of smoke
evolving a language all its own   elk and swallow are

images that populate the landscape   a slow and trailing line of ash
incommensurate in the time of writing   Witness

is a seraphim attached to a trail of graphite   smeared &
burning in the April night   heavenly as water on the

lips the angelic force moving across morning sky   White
trail of smoke in April   burden that burns one's genetic

make-up   Flowers at the gate   signs of ash on oak and elm
black rain from the April sky   Flowers at the gate no longer burning

A circle of forest   blue perimeter of swallows that defines
ash on white elms   swallows that rest inside a perimeter of white

ash in the forest   the purity of sight to select what is seen
in the forest   a single tree left at the edge   white elm edged

with ash   columnar structures at the edge of the visible
edged by forest that is no longer forest   gravesite

where forest was   blossoms of the sumac in water
the skies of Pripyat   charcoal on blue foam board

rim of the visitation one makes   to ring the cycle
forest   swallow   tree   as if woven together

beneath skies offering no protection from ash & fire.

4

Possible to trace   not possible to say   degradation

of light in the forest   Red forest in a low wind

Light that follows from inside the forest   moves outside

a circle of branches   gathered on wet ground

this turning of ash and wind   aligned in the red forest

To rename what it was   wild boar and elk

in a field without trees   to rename their passing

fox and deer returning to a landscape   the language

alienated from itself   this partition inscribed in red

wood scent of air that remains   burnt limbs of the poplar tree

One moves inside the zone to find them   to re-situate

chronology inside a disrupted limb   the markings of fox

and rabbit moving inside a circle   ring of red leaves

on a brown background   in the red forest

swallows resuming their call   black spots

of light on the brown floor   sky becomes an agent

of change   burning the river from both ends.

5

Lupine & flowering mullein where the road ends
spruce and hornbeam   lupine where the road disappears

in a circle of mullein and stevia   blue lid of sky
to transition from one world to another   not sky

where the road deepens   flowers that are a bridge
to the other side   stevia & sorghum at the forest's edge

How are we to say what was here?   First field of light
inside a perimeter   'zones of alienation'   lupine

& feather grass bordering an abandoned house   Blue
shutters on white stone   raised shelf of cowslip

Two are one   raised lupine & flowering mullein
form a chain of reflection   refractions of not-Eden

smooth face of white birch   dissolves in a slow
moving wind   shelter of mullein and feather grass

bald cypress low to the road   disappearing
under red skies   enfolded in flora from Lelyov

blue green skin of birch blackened by ash.

6

What was left not Eden but its refraction   not Eden
but its reflection   on cellophane the wrapped limbs of

radioactive logs   gathered in a line & placed on the mud
red inside a seam of green   the logs laid over ants

spiders bugs that lined the surface   granular surface
of sky poured over burning logs   wet to the touch

earth where they were laid   like fences arranged
on a wet landscape   Not Eden but its

aftermath   a chorus of children in a ring
of wire & light   caught at the edge of the red forest

swallows where a field was   wild boar & fox
moving toward the perimeter   in the alienation zone

where they have come to rest   Not Eden
inside a ring of white logs   placed in the landscape

end-to-end   as far as the eye can see   end-to-
end   in a trail of ash & smoke

swallows & sparrows moving inside the empty shell
of sarcophagus.

22 May –4 June 2019 / 1 March 2020

IV

In Place Of Conversation
for John Taggart

                    The central principle of any poetics
                    is that it ought to result in poetry.

1

Rising now to pre-dawn
      quadrants of yellow
   tags across the skyline.

The days begun in semi-darkness.

      One can't assess
   daylight by what it
           has yet to become—

Mornings as intimate
acts of retrieval—

    4 a.m.
Robins outside our window
   their song cycling
         in the dark.

2

Niedecker in a letter she sent
to Zukofsky (dated by LZ June 2,1946)—

       'One morning about 4:30
    I was partly awake but I knew I was
    hearing a bird I'd never heard—
    started with three deep churns and

        ended with some mild, ventriloquial
        flute notes. The end I recognized
        as wood thrush but had never heard
        the first but I told myself: now later
        keep in mind that this was real, I was
        awake, not dreaming…'

The unfamiliar tones mixed with the known…
as I am aware again

            through an open window.…of robin song and chickadee.

3

Working my way backward
to your response to Palmer in the
essay 'Were You' that serves as bridge
to your 'Rothko Chapel Poem'

    'un-name the beasts

    tear at his clothes
    keep throwing away, speed
    up the decay process'

Writing this in midst of a
global pandemic, destruction

moves without sound—

    intractable   visualized
  as public wounding
        this spell of wonder

    at the body's vulnerability.

4

There's parallelism   and relation
between   beginnings & endings

Poetry's elemental   track
raveled   wavy   unseen at this

distance   as you wrote 'whatever I
might have to say about loss & its relatives

is better said in poems'

5

I'm returning to   these pages
days later   certainty's long
ago   prospect   revised repeatedly—

     antecedent drafts   worked
along the grain of self's lone
                    itinerary

6

The realism of one to one...

Hearing you say it again, 'there are
birds...there are birds'

which becomes signatory for this spring
listening again   for the birds

to return   sparrow   robin   finch   nuthatch
from a window to watch the birds

returning in spring   not allegorical
birdsong across the yard

a day another day.

7

'The jump between fact
and the imaginative reality'

Williams writes
in *Spring and All*

'the wave rhythm
sliding into nothing'

Walking backward across the yard to pull
a few stray weeds up—

        crescent moon visible in the east
     facts of observation bordering
                  principles of reality.

8

There are things to do together and things to do by ourselves.

In late years to return to
these rituals of form. These

arrangements
that are also idioms

of survival—

Faceless outside
is one draft for another

to see.

9

Duration as light
is duration. Saturates

ground   river water
unseen   pours over the

lichen-covered rocks
of the Delaware....

    I wander the towpath   where the derelict Susquehanna
train car rests
 inside   sit awhile on metal posts for seats

    take a few minutes to get used to the light
        mixed with a breeze coming on...

10

Pausing to read Moore's 'Crossing
Brooklyn Bridge at Twilight' (1967)—noting
trees—English elms and sycamores—

    and the Williamsburg Savings Bank clock tower
        visible for miles...

11

Turned loose,
        you might say   waiting for rain.

The ground parched   you noted   not a
drop of rain in weeks…

12

A delay   then the pattern
of removal—

        Our neighbor
      gone two weeks—
                not coming back.

          'in the starlight things the things continue'

13

Walking east toward
town   routine to come back
            the same way—

Inside & outside commingle
       where the cemetery divides
     into separate sectors
          of the dead—

The earliest buried   in the northeastern quadrant.

Walking past rows of headstones
       from the 1840's   returning
  at the gate to enter Court Street
          the sharp afternoon light
  moving from the west.

14

    What gets into
the poem—

    ready or not

here it comes…

    An afterthought following
images of sun
        moving across the yard.

15

'Unsure of the times…'

    What stays new
here—the odd phases

of seeing break apart   essentials

    from another life—

    'I drink deeply
  to banish such thoughts

for awhile
then burst into song, so

terribly sad'

Our hands caressing
late birch pieces   cut after a

spring storm.

16

Each day   some
notes come back   foreign

familiar   lines from
Robin   'the words drink

us up / who is speaking?

dear beings, I can feel your hands'

17

Your words are this far   from my own
inside another landscape   written out of

no eyes but these   'daylight breaks
across the western hills   a soft rain is

beginning here   rain that is most
welcome   these long dry months without

water.'

18

      There's pantomime in water

  'look at the lily as bones as leaves and petals'

          ground breaks where the zone
      has been cut back
               to give us roses

19

The diction   to change
a world inside another's

world   'shades of meaning'
we are last to know

ourselves   to name what isn't
able to be named   Say it

via catachresis   as Miller
proposes in *The Ethics of Reading*

'only such a break   can effect
feeling in the self'

20

Books left on the shelf—

Virgil's plants brought
forward in a book left out

of doors   to arise
with its pages intact.

Genista…Spanish
or weaver's broom….

'The willow and humble
broom provide leafage

for the herd or shade
for shepherds.'

The branches are also
used for weaving

baskets….

21

The crystal
   held in our
             hands—

    as if
  you had offered
         it to us

    one night in
  Cumberland Valley
         far from

    water the days
  you offered us
         light & tea.

22

It's the difference between becoming & seeing....

To write through the days....Field
we have come to expect will

last forever. Nothing so impermanent
we can't read it back into this patchwork light

entering a field at sundown. You
would have understood the red

crease   the foil of linum bearing
signs of harvest. 'For a crop

of flax burns the soil.'

23

Keeping it all in—
        surface registers of experience

The poem as movement toward
                the light from across

As one mediates
from this distance

    pools in the open distance
  fold your arms
      & descend

24

'When the man writing is frightened by a word,
he may have started.'

Strange to wait
the majority of one's life for it

to begin.

25

      Reading Blackburn
to get the sense of it again
            so he saw himself

riding apart   a little day at a time
no daylight   but light sprung from inside

a clockface   I saw over the Williamsburg
Bank in Brooklyn   1988   I was walking

up Atlantic Ave.   to hit the bridge
moving as a body moves   mostly
            inside feints of light & shadow

26

Writing outside arcadia, you said
a saner approach might come.

A building....now & again crossing over
into that space where sound

became matter. You wrote
'red stairs lead us to three red rooms'

assumptive as the poem is
a record of our having come down

to ask the question again. *How
can we be in two places at once—*

*in our body
and not?*

27

Walking northeast to stop
        next to gravestones for the family of
                Cornelius, Jane and Sarah Shepherd (1797-1915)

while at the other end of the row
        the new dug gravesite awaits
                its owner.

Flowering this early spring...Apple
        blossom   & dogwood   lining
                a path.

One's hands go
        out to touch them   bright petals
                of magnolia at path's end.

28

'snowfall
around midnight
two of all the sycamore's trees remaining'

from your 'Pastorelle' series
copy of which I kept   years from our time

together   'One thinks

back to find a new line—'

29

Whosoever says   these dreams
kept you up   cherry and myrtle   opening

the door   there is the sound of
rain   storms from the west   out of earshot

30

'the reason for not writing is
to write—'

       all things clear   as the harbor reappears

  you said   this new-minted

        idiom   change of address
   as you would know…

31

My father's cherry
tree outside his Levittown apartment   his last spring

      so that he asked each day, 'Did
my cherries come?'

Abstract in recollection   the trees
in full bloom in early spring

outside a window   pink blooms
of *kwiaty wiśni*   falling to the ground.

32

Use this day   someone else's
day is coming back   shared beginnings
      of a walk we took   once farther than this

      Another's walking backward
    deep into the Ohio valley—

          Our body isn't anyplace
      at all you said just
          this once—set free.

33

We are starting
to combine   commingle

    elements left out
of the mix   Roses in a box
          garden   1962

Mint & rosemary
   mixed in their plot.

34

There is this re-tracing
   we say it's a pattern
      as children we

     danced to it   1-2-3
  waltz time   shoes left out
    doors—

   And our mother's
face—inside the door
    light—

from her room.   'The birds
sing'   someone moves inside
      —magnolia blossoms loose

   on slanted wood…

35

This is the space we can come
back to—
    black shaded Japanese maple

You wrote me of its
destruction after a storm   said

the damage was complete   'crushing

a viburnum'   that would recover

      After all   systems of care
emerge   take root in fall's
             pale moon rest

36

'bones as the ring bone as the ring of the flower'

      to carry legibility through the dark   like a child
   returning across   a ring of stones

         'far out of the world'   you looked up to see a the bank of
    Canadian geese flying

         unclouded parts of the sky.

37

Resting where he was
writing from—
      'the dead do read us'

Voices come in   go out
shorten   lengthen   the day-
      light   weakened

as if underwater. 'A special kind of seeing'
      Moore says, you need that 'rapture'
        that 'labor' to get there.

38

So that where we go
we are carried forward by these
              recognitions—

    'Heart's work' you said

keeps its distance….its inviolate
                           measure.

39

As Blaser tells us

Purgatory   'is the realm in which
  you are given the possibility
  of reclaiming love, any age
  of your life that has not known
  love, understood it, been able
  to act in it, since it is an action
  and nothing else but an action
  that will then finally return you
  to yourself…'

where we find ourselves again—
        rooted   unrooted   fateful
    to the last days   a person's hopefulness

speaking from inside the silence.

40

Anywhere you go   upland white aster

seen from the road   low across an eastern fence

      in early summer to see their blooms

    linear oblong   smooth green   ray flowers

of ten to twenty in each head…white….pappus white…

41

Robin wrote 'with
   excitement in the
             conversation'

  inscribed in my copy of
       The Holy Forest (Coach
           House edition)

 Our first and only
         meeting, 17 April 1994—

intact as his instructions were
        from that world to this

      'Language is love'

42

      The room opens out   onto the desert (you wrote words left out)

where the meeting happened   you said it was grace made it fall
             tree limb in the back
                           yard you said it was

      limb going to fall in a yard   after the rain storm

            you came back inside the room   saw it wasn't there

   Japanese maple snapped in a garden   out back

43

'The sound of the rain is whooshing….mud
        befouls this august Earth—when will it ever dry'

44

 'I drop in to say
hello….passing by chance

the door of another's
house'

What was said I
can't recall—

'guided by water and sky'

a slow waking
body   returns or doesn't

say a thing

       a design to signify / these patterns
   of resolve   located at the water's
                            edge

45

From another chapter
we saved time   to come here

          voices opening out
              to your chapel

46

Fall's valley   slow falling

branches   laid one to

one—

              Days come back   intervening periods
        of cloud and light

                      breaking the field in two.

47

To go down
        'is a fearful thing'

where you go

is where you

go to....

48

At rest, John
I meant our world was
    never without this

    inside or out
kept to ourselves while
    learning to talk

        among strangers.

49

        Everything we thought to say
            before us—

    'wind   roots   seed   the tree'

        held in mind...

50

        To gather up we said
        there were these sticks

        we have put them into
        a pile   now gather them

        up again   put them in a
        pile   after it will be

        the season   turning inside this
        'taut weave of consciousness'

51

Astonished
    to see days
              held by this music.

So can it be
so often the day is
        less than

we thought—

      Rites of passage
or the aftermath
        of other

      days—weaker
from having been
        restored

      'listen to the bones   they
have made your name   sweet'

52

      where the gathering is done   quickly   without premeditation
or fore-thought   lines' signatory appeal   that they make a home
            inside the poem   a sanctuary for song

going as we go   across the landscape   to see the terms of each
new season
          passing in real time.

53

As you wrote   'the last blackness
where the roots are / where the words' roots are'

Your book in its slipcase   saved among
early gatherings   to remain inside

the contours of each line

'until the secret parent appears'

One's life becomes a summa of these
separations   spring & fall   held by the hands

of strangers.

27 February-3 April 2020

Afterword

'Surroundings answer questions,' John Taggart has proposed. Which is to say we need to discover the questions to ask of those surroundings, their meaning and purpose in our lives. These poems travel back and forth between sites, places, states that are geographical realities and imaginal constructs proposing new questions that must be answered. The core geographies of my lifetime come forward in these poems as elements of both a material and spiritual autobiography. They exert pressure on this day—and all the days before them—this present—and all the presents before this one—even as they represent locales and histories long since past.

Here I go back inside spirit's house that is at once the province of deep lore and a lingual space of entrancement, meeting, re-inscription. 'My mind plays in the distance,' Robin Blaser writes, 'free, but not mine.' So that I might remember what the poem is, a co-creation with those who accompany me there, the tutelary figures who come forward in the writing. In the world of the poem, language teaches us to follow. We see what the language lets us see. Form is the bridge. 'The poet has no part in being,' Blaser continues in the same poem, 'is not the priest of ontology.' These poems are an account of where the language has led me, in a séance of mind and body in which we attend on the dead who read back to us what we've written.

Doylestown, PA
15 April 2020

Notes

MOON CYCLE: 'The dead, awaiting these visitors' is from Rachel Blau DuPlessis, *Late Work*. 'At the foot of a chessboard' is from Józef Czapski, *Lost Time: Lectures on Proust in a Soviet Prison Camp*. 'I remain fixed on myself' is from Witold Gombrowicz, *Diaries 1953-1969*. The lines from Du Fu are from *The Poetry of Du Fu*, translated by Stephen Owen. Descriptions of flowers are from *Wild Flowers* by Homer D. House (Macmillan Company 1934).

THE ELEMENTS: Jeremy Davies' *The Birth of the Anthropocene* was the source text for certain phrases and words that appear in this poem.

THE FIRE CYCLE: Texts that informed this poem's writing include Svetlana Alexievich's *Voices from Chernobyl: The Oral History of a Nuclear Disaster* (translated by Keith Gessen), Robert Polidori's *Zones of Exlucison: Prpyat and Chrnobyl*, and Alla Yaroshinskaya's *Chernobyl* (translated by Michèle Kahn and Julia Sallabank).

CITY EARTH: This poem draws on a number of texts related to the work of the environmental artist, Michael Heizer, including *Effigy Tumuli: The Reemergence of Ancient Mound Building* and *Double Negative*.

LINES IN PLACE OF CONVERSATION: John Taggar's *Is Music* and *There Are Birds* were the source texts for many of the phrases and lines that appear, sometimes unmarked, in this poem. 'In the starlight things the things continue' is from George Oppen, as is 'When a man is frightened by a word,' from a letter to Rachel Blau DuPlessis, October 21, 1965. The citation from Moore is from her *Collected Prose*. 'I drink deeply to banish such thoughts' and 'The sound of the rain is whoosing' are from *The Poetry of Du Fu*. The Blaser quote on Purgatory appears in *The Astonishment Tapes* and is quoted from Miriam Nichols's *A Literary Biography of Robin Blaser*. The line beginning 'wind   roots' is from Larry Eigner, *shape shadow element move*, Sparrow 13, Black Sparrow Press, October 1973.

Acknowledgements

THE FIRE CYCLE and CITY EARTH originally appeared in *Conjunctions 73: Earth Elegies*. My thanks to Bradford Morrow for his support of this work. Especial gratitude to Tod Thilleman who made substantive comments on earlier drafts of this book that have been integrated into the text as it appears here. For her insights and careful reading of a late draft of this book, I am deeply grateful to Rachel Blau DuPlessis. Her contributions were likewise invaluable in helping me revise this work into its final form. To Monica, who read every word and gave this book its initial shape and direction, I owe my profoundest thanks. This book is dedicated to her with love.

ANDREW MOSSIN is the author of five previous books of poetry: *The Epochal Body* (2004), *The Veil* (2012), *Exile's Recital* (2014), *Torture Papers* (2016), and *Songs for the Preparation of Perception* (2017). He is also the author of a collection of critical essays, *Male Subjectivity and Poetic Form in "New American" Poetry* (2010). He is an Associate Professor in the Intellectual Heritage Program at Temple University in Philadelphia. He lives in Doylestown, PA.

www.ingramcontent.com/pod-product-compliance
Lightning Source LLC
Chambersburg PA
CBHW030155100526
44592CB00009B/295